Weather

KINGFISHER
NEW YORK

KINGFISHER
LONDON & NEW YORK

Copyright © Kingfisher 2012
Book concept copyright © Toucan Ltd. 2012
Illustrations copyright © Simon Basher 2012

Published in the United States by Kingfisher,
175 Fifth Ave., New York, NY 10010
Kingfisher is an imprint of Macmillan Children's Books, London.
All rights reserved.

Consultant: Dr. Peter Inness, University of Reading, U.K.

Designed and created by Basher www.basherbooks.com
Text written by Dan Green

Dedicated to Simon Marbrook

Distributed in the U.S. and Canada by Macmillan,
175 Fifth Ave., New York, NY 10010

Library of Congress Cataloging-in-Publication data has been applied for.

ISBN: 978-0-7534-6825-8

Kingfisher books are available for special promotions and premiums.
For details contact: Special Markets Department, Macmillan,
175 Fifth Ave., New York, NY 10010.

For more information, please visit www.kingfisherbooks.com

Printed in China
9 8 7 6 5 4 3 2 1
1TR/0512/WKT/UG/140MA

CONTENTS

Introduction
Weather

Whatever weather you're having right now, it is bound to be the subject of conversation. People just love to talk about the weather! Did you know that there are some places on this planet where the weather doesn't change much from day to day? People living there wake up and put on the same kinds of clothing every morning. Yet in other places, not only is the weather variable from one day to the next, but it can even change dramatically in the course of 24 hours! First it's sunny, then it's rainy, then it's windy, then it's rainy again . . . In these places, folks need an entire closet full of clothes and a suitcase of stuff just to get from one end of the day to the next!

One thing that seems certain about this weather of ours (besides the fact that it's tricky to forecast) is that it is changing. That's right! In your lifetime, the weather is going to get very, very interesting. There are things happening with the world's climates right now, and the Extreme Weather crew is trying to get more of a look-in. You need to get to know these guys and their fair-weather friends. Come on—let's meet them.

Weather

Chapter 1
World of Weather

This powerful bunch has taken the world by storm. Some of these high rollers have an impact that influences the entire planet, and many of them are large-scale weather systems. The Sun is the boss, as its energy makes all of Earth's weather. Yearly cycles, such as the Seasons, Monsoon, and (to a lesser extent) El Niño, are created by the angle at which the planet orbits the Sun. The tilt is so great that, in the winter, the poles remain constantly in Earth's shadow, facing away from the Sun, and so receive no sunlight. In the summer, the polar regions become "lands of the midnight sun" and have no night.

Sun

Seasons

Climate

Monsoon

El Niño

Forecast

Weather
Satellite

Climate
Change

Sun

World of Weather

- ☀ The center of the solar system, this dude is our closest star
- ☀ Provides energy to drive climate, weather, and life on Earth
- ☀ This early riser shines a bright light that we call "day"

Good morning! I am the brightest thing in the sky. I dazzle when Earth turns on its axis to face me, and I outshine everything. I have the power to make you smile, or even make you want to take your clothes off! But that's nothing compared to the effects I have on gassy Atmosphere.

I'm simply bursting with energy—visible light, radio and infrared waves, ultraviolet waves, x-rays, gamma rays—you name it. I pump out this energy, and it hurtles through space, crossing the 93 million mi. (150 million km) from me to Earth in just eight minutes, 19 seconds flat. It smashes into that wet blanket Atmosphere, driving moisture off land and sea to form fluffy Cloud. My energy heats the air, but unevenly, creating pressure differences that mix and churn up Atmosphere, so triggering Earth's wild weather.

- ● Surface temperature of the Sun: 10,300 °F (5,700 °C)
- ● Highest recorded temperature on Earth: 136 °F (57.8 °C) (El Azizia, Libya, 1922)
- ● Sunniest place: Yuma, Arizona (4,000 hours of sunshine per year)

Sun

Seasons
World of Weather

⁕ Four periods dividing the year—winter, spring, summer, fall
⁕ Each has its unique weather patterns and daylight hours
⁕ Caused by changes in Earth's position in regard to the Sun

We're a wacky crew. It's our slant on life that makes spring change to summer and fall to winter during the 12 months that Earth takes to race around Sun.

Earth's big, round belly (the equator) receives the greatest intensity of sunshine, because its surface is square on to hotshot Sun. Areas farther away from the equator get a more spread-out dose of Sun's energy, because the surface slopes away. At the same time, Earth orbits Sun at an angle of 23.5°, which means that one hemisphere is always receiving more direct energy than the other—and has summer while the other is having winter. The fact that Earth's orbit is elliptical (oval shaped), not circular, just adds to this effect. All in all, it's thanks to us that you always know whether to wear a woolly hat or shorts!

● Summer solstice: the longest day of the year
● Winter solstice: the shortest day of the year
● Equinox: one of two days in the year when night and day are roughly equal

Seasons

Climate

■ World of Weather

☀ The typical weather for a region over a long period of time
☀ Affected by latitude, height, and closeness to water
☀ Normally measured as an average of weather over 30 years

I'm The General, a grand planner poised over maps and charts. I'm not content to deal with the here and now, I take the long view. I present the bigger picture.

While weather is about Atmosphere's activity at present—if it's sunny or rainy, windy, cloudy, or dry—I deal with the behavior of the weather over time. I give a reliable picture of what the weather is like at any time of year, year after year. Sure, it might be raining now, but if soggy old Rain fails to show up for months on end, a place has a dry climate. I vary depending on many factors. For example, equatorial regions are hot because of the latitude, but they may also be wet or dry. Oceans store and shift Sun's energy around the globe, so some areas are warmer than you might expect for their latitude—well, no one's perfect!

● Climate zones: tropical, monsoon, dry, warm, cool, and cold
● Wettest place: the Khasi Hills, India (about 472 in. (1,200cm) rain per year)
● Driest place: the Atacama Desert, Chile (less than 0.004 in. (0.1mm) rain per year)

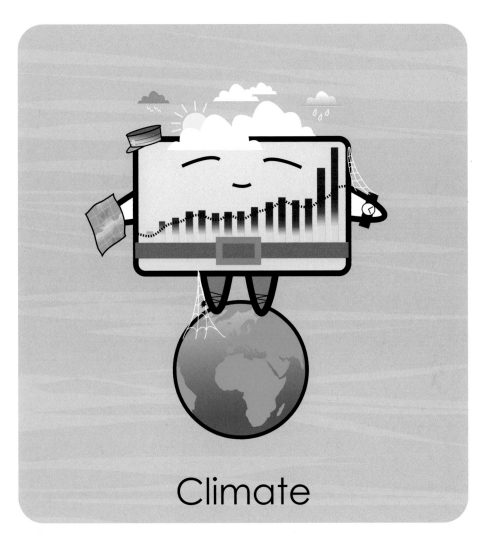

Climate

Monsoon

☀ A weather system of two seasons—rainy and dry
☀ Marked by a switch of wind direction and a change in rainfall
☀ Occurs in northern Australia, west Africa, south and east Asia

Boy, am I a big crybaby! Every year, I change from bright and sunny to sullen and sulky. I turn on the tears, instantly bringing cloudbursts of my favorite play pal, Rain.

So, why am I so wet? Well, in the winter, the ocean stays warm for longer than the land does. The air overlying the land cools and sinks, creating a zone of high pressure that drives winds from the land out across the ocean. But in the summer, the land heats up quicker than the ocean, and the cycle reverses. Now, as the warm air over land rises, it draws in water-laden air from the ocean. This air rises, too, shedding my violent rain bursts as it cools. I am a great provider of fresh water—vital for healthy crops. But I can also be deadly, dumping so much water onto land that Flood shows up. The thought brings me close to tears . . .

● First monsoon: about 15 to 20 million years ago
● Wettest mountains: 118–157 in. (300–400cm) of rain per year (Western Ghats, India)
● The summer monsoon accounts for more than 80% of India's annual rainfall

Monsoon

El Niño
▪ World of Weather

✴ Upsets the normal interaction of the ocean and atmosphere
✴ Affects western coasts of North, South, and Central America
✴ El Niño is Spanish for "little boy"

I am your genuine tropical terror, a scamp that shows up every two to five years. I usually arrive around Christmastime, but I'm no welcome present, I can tell you!

I tamper with the normal conditions of the Pacific Ocean. What's normal, you say? Well, trade winds at the equator push water westward across the Pacific to Indonesia and Australia. Cold water rises up from the depths to replace the water shifted across the surface. With it come nutrients that make the East Pacific superb for fishing. Perfect . . . until I come along, that is. I weaken gusty Wind, breaking the cycle. The warm water stays where it is, and the cold water does not rise. The effects on Atmosphere can be devastating: Drought parches the west, Rain and Flood swamp the east, and there are fewer fish. I love chaos!

● Followed by La Niña, which reverses the conditions
● Upwelling: the movement of water from the depths of the ocean to its surface
● Average West Pacific sea level: 1.6 ft. (0.5m) higher than East Pacific sea level

El Niño

Forecast

* This guy uses scientific methods to predict the weather
* Has data gatherers, such as satellites and weather balloons
* Supplies information to aviation, shipping, and the military

Everyone's desperate to know what the weather's up to, and try to have all of the answers. Yep, I take real-time data from my vast team of gatherers, feed it into complex computer models . . . and hope for a reliable outlook. Hey, I'm dealing with nature here! I can be short range (tomorrow) or long range (a month). However, the longer the range, the less accurate I am. Bah!

Forecast

- First recorded forecasts: 650 B.C. (Babylonian)
- A rapid fall in pressure signifies that bad weather is coming
- Rising pressure suggests that more settled weather can be expected

Weather Satellite

World of Weather

* Orbits Earth and is used to monitor the weather
* Reveals a lot about global weather and climate
* An early-warning system of climate change

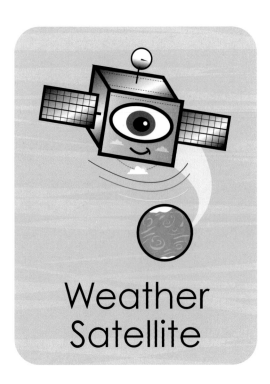

Weather Satellite

I'm a space-age marvel, circling endlessly, always watching. I keep my fully automatic unblinking eye on the weather. I monitor wind shifts and cloud formation. I zap data and pictures back to Earth for you to see on TV. But it's not all storms and clouds; I'm also something of a snitch when it comes to global warming. There's not much that vile Climate Change gets past me!

● Orbit height: 530–22,300 mi. (850–35,880km)
● The first-ever weather satellite, TIROS-1, was launched in 1960
● The Antarctic ozone hole was first observed by a weather satellite in 1984

Climate Change
■ World of Weather

* ✹ Flame-haired character currently causing global warming
* ✹ A bringer of extreme weather, such as floods and droughts
* ✹ Your "carbon footprint" is your own personal contribution

Let's face it, Earth is getting hotter. A lot of this is due to me, but no matter how many times I say it, there are still soooo many people who refuse to believe that I exist.

"Even Climate admits to being a little unpredictable," they say, and "Climate's been warmer in the past, you know." Yeah, right! I love you humans—there you go burning your fossil fuels (coal, oil, gas) and pumping your greenhouse gases into Atmosphere. Meanwhile, that big, stuffy blanket is getting very sticky with all of that extra heat it's trapping. The icecaps and glaciers are melting and sea levels are rising. I'm just itching for it all to get out of hand. You could reduce your personal energy usage and shift to cleaner, greener ways of producing power. But, hey, who's listening to me? I don't exist, remember!

* ● Average global temperature rise: 1.4 °F (0.8 °C) since 1900
* ● Main greenhouse gases: water vapor, carbon dioxide, methane
* ● 2000–2010 was the hottest decade in 400 years

Climate Change

Chapter 2

■ Blue-sky Dreamers

These guys are all up in the air. They may seem like a bunch of dreamers, but the stuff they get up to affects our daily weather. Meet Atmosphere who envelops Earth in its huge gassy blanket and plays host to these Blue-sky dudes. You'll find Jet Stream whizzing around here and Weather Front along for the ride. Cloud shows up when water vapor in the air reaches its dew point and forms liquid droplets. Things really get going when Wind blows in —you can *feel* Atmosphere then. Pressure's highs and lows reflect the shifting weight of Atmosphere's constantly moving gases, giving us clues to what's coming up . . .

Atmosphere

Pressure

Wind

Jet Stream

Cloud

Weather Front

Atmosphere

■ Blue-sky Dreamers

☀ The stuff that the sky is made from
☀ A blanket of gases that keeps us warm
☀ Causes the weather by spreading heat and water around

If *party* and *atmosphere* are words you like, look no further for the perfect host. Mine is a heady cocktail of four parts nitrogen to one part oxygen, with just a dash of argon. Life with me is a *gas*.

I'm an invisible marvel, wrapping around the world to keep it cozy and shielding life from a bombardment of lethal radiation from space. I have five layers. Rain, Hail, Cloud, and Weather Front all strut their stuff in my lower layer, the troposphere. The ozone layer is found above that in the stratosphere. Other gases spike my mix—nasty greenhouse gases that Climate Change brags about. They're present in tiny amounts but, boy, are they trouble! Pollen, volcanic ash, dust, and the pollutant sulfur dioxide also muscle their way in. It chokes me up to think about it.

● The layers: troposphere, stratosphere, mesosphere, thermosphere, exosphere
● Coldest part of the atmosphere: −148 °F (−100 °C) (mesosphere)
● Official boundary of Earth's atmosphere with space: 60 mi. (100km) up

Atmosphere

Pressure

Blue-sky Dreamers

- The weight of the gases in the atmosphere
- Measured using a barometer
- A change in pressure signals a shift in the weather

You've probably heard the expression "as light as air," but that's just part of it. What goes up must come down— that's my motto. I'm an up-and-down kind of guy!

When people talk about me, they mean the weight of all of the air over an area of land or ocean. Imagine a tall column of air rising up into the sky. The higher you get in the column, the less air there is above you, pressing down. This is why the pressure drops when you rise in an airplane or climb a mountain. Atmosphere's gases are constantly shifting, and I change with them. I have highs and lows, but they are not like your uplifting highs and heavy, heavy lows. Instead, air sinks over an area of land with high pressure, while low pressure makes the opposite happen—it causes the air to rise. Up, up, and away . . .

- Average sea-level pressure: 101.325 kPa (kilopascals)
- Highest recorded atmospheric pressure: 108.57 kPa (Mongolia, 2001)
- Lowest recorded: 85 kPa, in the center of a tornado (South Dakota, 2003)

Pressure

Wind

■ Blue-sky Dreamers

❋ Huffs and puffs to move air masses around
❋ Blows from high-pressure zones to low-pressure zones
❋ Winds that blow most of the time are called trade winds

I like to get things movin'. I wanna see trees dancin' and hats tumblin'. I can be very slight—a breath of air—or I can rage. My storm force whips tiles off roofs, flings cars around, and snaps branches. When I blow, you feel Atmosphere press against you. Because I shift air around, I also move water and heat. Temperatures feel lower than they really are when I'm around. *Brrr!*

Wind

● Trade winds: steady easterly winds that blow across the Earth's tropical oceans
● Windiest place: Commonwealth Bay, Antarctica (up to 300 mph (322km/h))
● Highest recorded cyclonic wind speed: 254 mph (408km/h) (Australia, 1996)

Jet Stream

Blue-sky Dreamers ■

* ✷ This high-altitude, high-speed wind usually flows east
* ✷ Found around Earth's poles and subtropical regions
* ✷ Can create a weather front and drive it forward

Jet Stream

Anchors aweigh! Strap on those flying goggles and follow my narrow currents as they snake around Earth at high speed. Isn't it every guy's fantasy to fly with the real jets in the cool stratosphere, way up above the planet? Well, I'm up there, baby, looking down on my fellow Blue-sky pals. You don't want to mess with me, though. Planes that go against my flow could suffer delays!

* ● Jet-stream height: 4–7 mi. (7–12km): polar jets; 6–10 mi. (10–16km): subtropical jets
* ● Typical size of jet stream: few hundred mi. wide; 3 mi. (5km) deep
* ● Jet-stream speed: 125–250 mph (200–400km/h)

Cloud

■ Blue-sky Dreamers

- ✴ Large collection of water droplets or ice crystals in the sky
- ✴ Occurs when air cools and water vapor turns to liquid
- ✴ One of the best indicators of weather to come

Wandering high and lonely, I'm a dreamy fellow. Poets and folks who stare at the sky go all wishy-washy about me, but there's more to me than my soft, pillowy looks.

In fact, I'm pretty gray and damp—a mass of swirling water vapor. My different forms are classed by shape and height in Atmosphere's lowest level, the troposphere, which is where I hang out. Wispy cirrus floats its boat very high up, and coming down to Earth, you'll find puffy white cumulus, graying alto types, blanketlike stratus, and rain-bearing nimbus. My forms often combine: stratocumulus is the round, gray-hulled cloud you get on a cloudy-with-sunny-patches kind of day, while nimbo-stratus is dark and leaden. If you see me getting lower in the sky, Weather Front is on its way. Run for cover!

- ● Inventor of cloud classification: Luke Howard (1803)
- ● Amount of Earth's water in clouds: 0.035%
- ● Airplanes that fly through clouds often experience turbulence

Cloud

Weather Front

■ Blue-sky Dreamers

☀ This bad boy brings a change in the wind and weather
☀ Happens when cold and warm air masses meet
☀ Passes overhead in 24 hours and keeps moving for days

I'm a pushy little fellow that comes about when two air masses meet but refuse to mingle. Say they have a different density (one is lighter than the other)—they jostle and circle each other but never mix.

I create a boundary between a cold air mass and a warm one whenever one approaches the other. A heavy cold air mass will undercut a warm one, barging through to get ahead, while a lighter warm air mass simply sits on top of a cold one, forcing it out of the way. I can last for days as they battle it out, each bringing in fresh supplies, and I take my direction from speedy Jet Stream. It's at times like these that you'll find the weather happening. Wind, Cloud, Rain, Snow, Tornado, and Thunderstorm all try to get a look-in if they can. They have some "front!"

● Warm front on a weather map: red semicircles
● Cold front on a weather map: blue triangles
● Occluded front: when a warm front meets a cold one

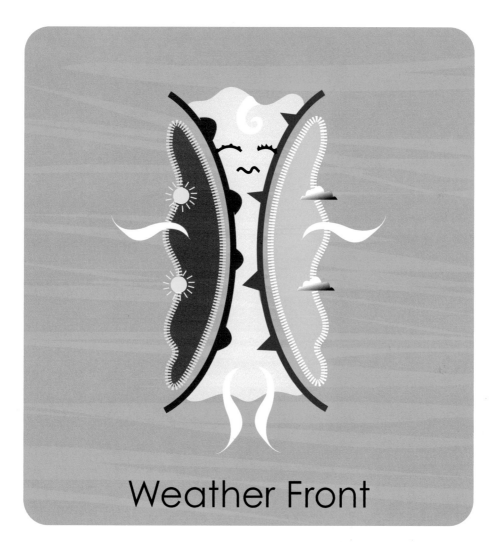

Weather Front

Chapter 3
■ Wet 'n' Wild

Here we have a pretty steamy bunch—the Wet 'n' Wild members of the weather world. They all have something to do with the way in which air holds water vapor. You already know that warm air holds more water vapor than cold air. You also know that warm air rises, but here's the rub: as a mass of warm air rises, it cools down. Its vapor condenses (turns into liquid water), which then falls back down to Earth as precipitation. What you need to worry about is whether it falls as a liquid (Rain) or a solid (Snow and Hail). Either way, you'd better look out, because you're likely to get soaking wet, freezing cold, or both!

Rain

Snow

Hail

Fog

Frost

Rainbow

Rain
■ Wet 'n' Wild

✳ Liquid precipitation that causes blue feelings and worse . . .
✳ Made when air holding water vapor cools
✳ A raindrop is shaped more like a burger bun than a teardrop

People treat me like I'm some kind of party pooper. The moment I gather, all gray and cloudy above their heads, I hear nothing but moaning and groaning. What a bunch of washouts! You know better than that, I'm sure. *You* know that I bring much-needed water to the land and that Earth rejoices at my arrival.

I tumble out of Cloud when water droplets or ice crystals get too heavy to hang suspended in the air. It all starts with the rising of warm air and its vapor, which turns from gas to liquid as it rises. But lovely Cloud has told you this already! If it gets colder, the water droplets emerging from the air start to clump together. If it's really cold (as it often is), ice crystals form. Soon poor Cloud bursts and I drop all the way back to Earth, melting as I fall. Splish splash!

● Speed of falling rain: up to 11 mph (18km/h)
● Global average annual rainfall: 39 in. (990mm)
● Most rain in one day: 70 in. (1,778mm) (Réunion, Indian Ocean, 1952)

Rain

Snow
■ Wet 'n' Wild

✳ Solid, icy precipitation; individual crystals of frozen water
✳ This beauty comes in many shapes and sizes
✳ Can be dry or wet, depending on air temperature

Everyone loves ME! Delicate and oh so pretty, I'm "snow" much fun to play in. Next time you make a snowball, just think—no two flakes of mine are the same. Incredible but true: each of the millions and billions of snowflakes lying around and falling from the sky is as individual as you!

You'd better wrap up warm when I'm swirling around. I'm the chilly stuff that happens when Rain doesn't quite manage to melt on its way down from Cloud. Since I am made of individual ice crystals, I am extremely light and fluffy. Gusty Wind whisks me here and there, building me up in drifts in sheltered corners where I come to rest. The air spaces between my crystals compress when you walk on a bed of me, which makes me squeak and creak. Cute? Heck, yes, but a heavy fall of me causes havoc!

● Average speed of falling snow: 3 ft. (1m)/sec.
● Largest snowfall (1 storm): 189 in. (480cm) (Mount Shasta Ski Bowl, California, 1959)
● Number of words for snow in the Sami languages of northern Europe: 300

Snow

Hail

Wet 'n' Wild

* Extreme form of solid precipitation; frozen balls of ice
* Formed in cold cumulonimbus storm clouds
* Collisions in clouds build up static electricity to make lightning

A real bruiser, I hammer on roofs and strip crops bare. I form in tall storm clouds, where strong updrafts shoot water droplets up into the air. Layers of ice build around each drop, and so I am born! Up, up I go, growing bigger and meaner with each new coat of ice. Once I'm too heavy for the updraft to support me, I plummet all the way down to Earth . . . and destruction.

Hail

● Hailstone size: 0.2–6 in. (0.5–15cm)
● Hailstone speed (a hailstone of 0.4 in. (1cm)): 30 ft. (9m)/sec.
● World's heaviest hailstone: 2 lb. (1kg) (Gopalganj, Bangladesh, 1986)

Fog
Wet 'n' Wild

* Ground-hugging cloud and close cousin of mist and smog
* Forms when cold air is trapped beneath a warm air mass
* Disappears in the blink of an eye when things heat up

Fog

I'm a wet blanket! I love to wrap things in my damp embrace. You'll find me lurking wherever water-vapor-laden warm air hits a chilly spot. Cooling rapidly, vapor condenses out of the air as millions of tiny droplets of dangling liquid water, AKA me, Fog. I love to torment drivers, pilots, and ships' captains, literally blinding them with my mysterious misty looks. So, who's wet now?!

* Official definition: when visibility is reduced to less than 0.6 mi. (1km)
* World's foggiest place: Grand Banks, Newfoundland, Canada
* Water content: less than 1.5 gal. (5.7L) in 1 cu. mi. (4km³) of fog

Frost

■ Wet 'n' Wild

☀ Ice that forms at ground level, made from frozen dew
☀ Occurs when the land is colder than the air
☀ This wintry fellow kills off plants

Cold and cruel, I creep around the place at night, freezing the ground, cars, trees, windows, and roofs with my icy touch. My sharp nip can mean death to many a plant hanging onto life as fall turns. And I'll bite any silly veggies that start growing too early in the spring.

It takes a special kind of magic to bring me out. When fiery Sun sets, the ground quickly loses the heat of the day. Water vapor in the warm air condenses on contact with the cold land and dewdrops appear. If it is below freezing, this dew forms chilly old me—glistening ice crystals that coat any surface upon which they land. Depending on the conditions, I appear in different guises. As hoarfrost, I occur on especially chilly nights. I'm so white and thick, you might think I'm that flake, Snow.

● Slight frost: 25.7–32 °F (–3.5 to 0 °C)
● Moderate frost: 20.3–25.5 °F (–6.5 to –3.6 °C)
● Severe frost: 11.3–20.1 °F (–11.5 to –6.6 °C)

Frost

Rainbow

■ Wet 'n' Wild

☀ A curving band of color in the sky, found opposite the Sun
☀ Occurs when light shines through droplets of water in the air
☀ Often seen in the spray coming from waves or waterfalls

Mine is a multicolored magic that brings a smile to your face. My looping bands of bright color are made by two bittersweet pals of mine—Rain and Sun.

My hero, Isaac Newton, was the genius who discovered how I came to exist and why my lovely colors always appear in the same order. You see, when light enters a drop of rain, it slows down just enough for the different frequencies bundled up inside white light to split. The light bounces off the back of the raindrop and is reflected in all of its glory as red, orange, yellow, green, blue, indigo, and violet. Because I'm a purely optical phenomenon, you can chase me, but you'll never find the point at which I touch the ground—the rainbow's end. The same can be said about that pot of gold. It just ain't there!

● Longest-lasting rainbow: 3 hours (Gwynedd, Wales, 1979)
● Memory aid for rainbow colors: ROY G BIV
● Angle of reflection inside a raindrop: 40–42°

Rainbow

Chapter 4
Extreme Weather

Be wary of this wild bunch! A group of freak weather conditions, these characters have a mean streak a mile wide. They are awesomely powerful—without so much as breaking a sweat, they can swat cars, sweep away roads and bridges, and make matchsticks out of houses. Normally, you barely feel the weight of the air, but this group shows you exactly the punch that Atmosphere can pull when it's stirred up. Scientists worry that global warming is making these guys more common. While they are certainly breathtaking to behold, let's be thankful that they don't come knocking more often . . . for now!

Thunderstorm

Lightning

Hurricane

Tornado

Ice Storm

Flood

Drought

Thunderstorm

■ Extreme Weather

☀ Booming bruiser that brings rain, hail, lightning, and thunder
☀ Formed in tall, anvil-shaped cumulonimbus clouds
☀ Thunder is a shock wave that rumbles out after a lightning bolt

Full of boisterous bluster, I bring strong winds and wild weather. Not a day goes by without me bursting my seams above some place or other on this planet.

I'm most likely to occur on hot, humid days, when warm, moist air surges upward into the sky. In the same way that Cloud comes about, the warm air cools and the water vapor turns into liquid. But updrafts keep my clouds building up until they are monsters, sometimes more than 12 mi. (20km) high! So strong are the updrafts that they shoot moisture-laden air right to the top of the troposphere, where it flattens out and forms my ominous anvil shape. Well, I can take only so much, and it's only a matter of time before I start lashing down Rain and flashing Lightning! Don't blame me—it's lonely up there!

● Number of thunderstorms happening right now: about 1,800
● Height of a typical thundercloud: 5–6 mi. (8–10km)
● Distance in mi.: number of seconds between lightning and thunder divided by 5

Thunderstorm

Lightning
■ Extreme Weather

☀ Sudden burst of electricity from clouds
☀ Can be sheet (cloud-to-cloud) or forked (cloud-to-ground)
☀ Always takes the quickest route to Earth

I'm a real flashy dude! I light up the sky with my electric moves. My bolts heat air about three times hotter than Sun's surface. The energy released in just one bolt is enough to toast about 100,000 slices of bread. Sizzle!

I thrive on Thunderstorm's turbulence. Water droplets, ice crystals, and dust bump and jostle in the updrafts and downdrafts, creating a static charge. I can equalize the charge by leaping between clouds as sheet lightning. But sometimes I discharge to the ground. First, I send out a negatively charged stream of electrically charged air. This encourages a positively charged feeler to rise up from any high point on Earth. As soon as the two connect, I discharge with full force. This return stroke is what you see as lightning. I'm one sparky guy, I tell you!

● Lightning bolt speed: 140,000 mph (220,000km/h)
● Heat of air around a lightning bolt: 54,000 °F (30,000 °C)
● Average number of lightning storms globally: 16 million per year

Lightning

Hurricane

■ Extreme Weather

✳ Weather system that brings strong winds and very heavy rain
✳ The center, or eye, of a hurricane is very low in pressure
✳ Also known as tropical cyclone and typhoon

Brooding and sulking, I'm an angry tiger of moist air, chasing my tail. Self-pitying Thunderstorm is a mere cub compared to me. My might is truly awesome! Mwahaha!

I form out at sea when Sun evaporates colossal quantities of water off the surface. The rising air and condensing water vapor build up a massive swirling heat engine that spirals counterclockwise in the Northern Hemisphere and clockwise in the Southern Hemisphere. Driven by Earth's rotation and steering winds, I set off on my trail of wild destruction—my eye calm and warm, yet surrounded by huge walls of menacing clouds. Around and around I go, causing havoc and uprooting anything in my path. Fellow extremist Flood bursts forth from my heavy rains and storm surges to maximize my terrifying potential for disaster.

● Deadliest hurricane: more than 300,000 killed (Bhola cyclone, Bangladesh, 1970)
● Strongest hurricane: 192 mph (310km/h) wind speeds (Typhoon Tip, 1979)
● Longest-lasting hurricane: 31 days (Hurricane John, Pacific Ocean, 1994)

Hurricane

Tornado
■ Extreme Weather

☀ A spinning tube of air, its wind speed is impossible to measure
☀ Reaches down from a thundercloud to the ground
☀ Travels an unpredictable path, creating chaos

C'mon, everybody, let's do the twist! I love to dance, and I long to pick you up and spin you around. But, to be honest, I know I'll just trash the place!

Responsible for some of the highest wind speeds on Earth, I'm about as extreme as weather gets. Coming out from the bottom of a cumulonimbus thundercloud, I hit the ground running, tossing cars around and smashing up houses. When I cross water, I suck it up into huge towers called waterspouts. (I've been known to make it rain frogs and fish!) I often take a turn in Tornado Alley, between the Rocky and Appalachian mountains. Most days, I run out of puff quickly, but every now and then, I get on a roll. The 2011 Super Outbreak made as many as 322 tornadoes in three days.

● Longest tornado travel: 219 mi. (352km) (Tri-State Tornado, 1925)
● Longest tornado duration: about 3.5 hours (Tri-State Tornado, 1925)
● Fastest forward speed: 73 mph (117km/h) (Tri-State Tornado, 1925)

Tornado

Ice Storm
■ Extreme Weather

☀ This malign pixie coats all surfaces in thick, slippery ice
☀ Strikes with hardly any warning when the conditions are right
☀ Also known as a glaze event and silver thaw

Merciless and mean, I freeze all that I touch. I love to cause utter mayhem, pulling down power lines and creating multicar pileups with my hard, icy glaze.

I'm a pretty rare event, although I seem to be occuring more frequently. It takes a certain kind of weather to bring me about: something I call an airy sandwich—a warm-air filling squished between two cold-air slices. Snow falling from the cold top layer melts as it passes through the warm middle part and then cools again as it falls through the cold bottom layer. Drops that don't turn to ice hit the already-frozen surface as supercooled water (below freezing point but not yet solid). The second they land, they solidify into hard ice, crusting heavily on power lines, pylons, roads, houses, and cars. Ice, ice, baby!

● Official ice-storm definition: 0.25 in. (0.64cm) of ice on exposed surfaces
● Power-line strain: 0.2 in. (0.6cm) of ice adds about 500 lb. (225kg) per line span
● Worst ice storm: 8 in. (20cm) of ice (Idaho, 1961)

Ice Storm

Flood

■ Extreme Weather

☀ Water overflow that damages buildings, roads, and sewers
☀ This big drip has devastating effects on low-lying areas
☀ Dependent on rainfall, storms, and climate

A soggy surplus of the wet stuff, I turn up when water bursts out of its normal channels. Fluid, creeping, and dangerous, my sudden, fast-flowing evil currents sweep people off their feet and away. I adore Hurricane's storm surges and the heavy rains that make rivers swell. Best of all, I love to catch Earth unawares; I flash across the land before it has time to soak me up.

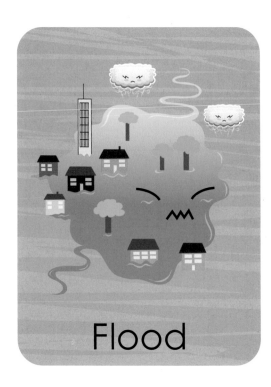

Flood

● Deadliest flood: 2,500,000 to 3,700,000 killed (Yellow River, China, 1931)
● World's largest flood defenses: the Netherlands
● Definition of a flash flood: occurs within a time scale of less than 6 hours

Drought

Extreme Weather ■

* ☀ Extended dry period without rain; often causes crops to fail
* ☀ Brought on by climate in dry regions (e.g. the Horn of Africa)
* ☀ Can lead to deforestation, erosion, and desertification

Drought

I am ying to Flood's yang. A sustained period of fine weather might sound promising but don't be fooled. I bring terrible dry spells that parch the land. Believe me, life without water is unpleasant. Vital crops and livestock perish and starvation looms. And once I'm in, I'm hard to move: I drive moisture from the ground, leaving not a drop to supply fresh rainfall. It's thirsty work!

* ● Deadliest drought: an estimated 9,000,000 deaths (China, 1876–1879)
* ● Proportion of Earth's land surface that is dry land: 41%
* ● Area affected by "Dust Bowl" drought (1930–1936): 154,000 sq. mi. (400,000km²)

Index

Character entries are **bold.**

MN
Monsoon 6, 12, **14**
Newton, Isaac 44

O
orbits 6, 10, 19, 63
ozone 24, 63, 64
ozone hole 63

P
poles 6, 29, 63
precipitation 34, 36, 38,
  40, 63
Pressure 8, 14, 18, 22, **26**,
  28, 52

R
radio waves 8, 64
Rain 12, 14, 16, 24, 30,
  32, 34, **36**, 38, 44, 48, 52,
  54, 58, 59
Rainbow **44,** 64

S
Seasons 6, **10**
Snow 32, 34, **38**, 42, 56
solar system 8, 64
spring 10, 42
storms 28, 32, 40, 50, 52,
  56, 58

storm surges 52, 58, 64
subtropical regions 29, 64
summer 6, 10, 14
Sun 6, **8**, 10, 12, 42, 44, 50, 52

T
thunder 48, 54
Thunderstorm 32, **48**, 50, 52
Tornado 32, **54**
trade winds 16, 28
tropical regions 12, 16, 28,
  52, 64

UV
ultraviolet waves 8, 64
updrafts 40, 48, 50, 64
visible light 8, 64

W
Weather Front 22, 24, 29,
  30, **32**
Weather Satellite 18, **19**
weather systems 6, 52
white light 44, 64
Wind 12, 14, 16, 19, 22, **28**,
  29, 32, 38, 48, 52, 54
winter 6, 10, 14

X
x-rays 8, 64

Glossary

Air mass A vast body of air of one density (at the same temperature and with the same water vapor content). When two air masses of different densities meet, they do not mix but form a weather front.

Altitude The height above sea level.

Axis An imaginary line around which things rotate. Earth spins around an axis that connects the two poles.

Carbon footprint The amount of carbon released into the atmosphere as a result of an activity or process; a figure used to compare the energy consumed to make or do something.

Cyclonic When wind travels in a fluid circular motion, rotating in the same direction as Earth.

Deforestation The felling of trees and changing of forest land into farmland or an urban zone.

Density Mass per unit volume; normally the amount of material in a given chunk of stuff.

Desertification The changing of land into dry land, often the result of climate change or owing to overfarming.

Downdraft Air moving vertically downward; descending air currents within clouds and areas of low pressure.

Equator An imaginary line around Earth, equidistant from the North and South poles and perpendicular to Earth's axis.

Erosion The wearing away of land by water, wind, and other natural processes.

Frequency The rate at which something repeats itself; the number of cycles it makes per second. The different colors found in white light are made of light waves of different frequencies.

Gamma ray Electromagnetic radiation of very high frequency (higher frequency than x-rays).

Greenhouse gas Any gas in the atmosphere that traps infrared waves and stops them from escaping Earth.

Hemisphere One half of the Earth; divided into northern and southern halves by the equator.

Infrared wave Low-frequency electromagnetic radiation, felt as heat.

La Niña A weather phenomenon in the Pacific Ocean that has the reverse effects as El Niño.

Latitude Imaginary lines around Earth, parallel to the equator. High latitudes are near the poles; low latitudes are near the equator.

Orbit The curved path of a planet around the Sun or a satellite around Earth.

Ozone hole Where the ozone layer in Earth's atmosphere becomes depleted owing to the effects of pollution.

Poles The two fixed points on Earth's surface where its axis intersects with the surface. The North Pole is the farthest point north and the South Pole the farthest south on Earth.

Precipitation Water that falls to Earth from the sky as rain, snow, sleet, or hail.

Glossary

Radiation Energy that travels as electromagnetic waves through space.

Radio wave Very low-frequency electromagnetic radiation; can be generated by lightning.

Solar system The family of planets, asteroids, and comets orbiting the Sun.

Storm surge When atmospheric pressure causes sea levels to rise during a storm.

Subtropical Relating to the regions next to the Tropics. Climate is milder here than in the Tropics, with hot summers but cooler winters.

Tropical The regions around the equator that mostly have a hot and humid climate but that can also be arid.

Ultraviolet wave Mid-frequency electromagnetic radiation that has a higher frequency than light. Ultraviolet waves can cause sunburn.

Updraft Air moving vertically upward; rising currents within clouds and areas of high pressure.

Visible light Mid-frequency electromagnetic radiation that the human eye can see.

White light Blended colors (frequencies) of light are perceived as white. This can be split by water droplets to form a seven-colored rainbow.

X-ray High-frequency electromagnetic radiation— higher frequency than ultraviolet waves but lower than gamma rays.